Simple Stitches: Sewing

D0536159

Simple Stitches: Sewing

25 Projects for the New Stitcher

CHERYL OWEN

An Imprint of Sterling Publishing Co., Inc.
New York
www.larkcrafts.com

Editor Clare Sayer
Photography Mark Winwood
Design Beverly Price, www.one2six.com
Production Laurence Poos
Editorial Direction Rosemary Wilkinson
Cover Design Megan Kirby

Reproduction by Modern Age Repro House Ltd, Hong Kong
Printed and bound in Singapore by Tien Wah Press (PTE) Ltd

Library of Congress Cataloging-in-Publication Data
Owen, Cheryl.
  Simple stitches. Sewing : 25 projects for the new stitcher / Cheryl Owen.—1st ed.
     p. cm.
  Includes index.
  ISBN 978-1-60059-905-7 (pb with flaps)
  1. Machine sewing. I. Title. II. Title: Sewing : 25 projects for the new stitcher.
  TT713.094 2010
  646.2—dc22

10 9 8 7 6 5 4 3 2 1

First Edition

Published by Lark Crafts, An Imprint of
Sterling Publishing Co., Inc.
387 Park Avenue South, New York, NY 10016

First Published in the UK 2011 by
New Holland Publishers (UK) Ltd
London • Cape Town • Sydney • Auckland
Text copyright © 2011: Cheryl Owens
Copyright © 2011 photographs and illustrations:
New Holland Publishers (UK) Ltd
Copyright © 2010 New Holland Publishers (UK) Ltd

Distributed in Canada by Sterling Publishing,
c/o Canadian Manda Group, 165 Dufferin Street
Toronto, Ontario, Canada M6K 3H6

If you have questions or comments about this book, please contact:
Lark Crafts
67 Broadway
Asheville, NC 28801
828-253-0467

Manufactured in Singapore

ISBN 13: 978-1-60059-905-7

For information about custom editions, special sales, premium and corporate
purchases, please contact Sterling Special Sales Department at 800-805-5489
or specialsales@sterlingpub.com.

For information about desk and examination copies available to college and
university professors, requests must be submitted to academic@larkbooks.com.
Our complete policy can be found at www.larkcrafts.com.

contents

Introduction

The craft of sewing has been hugely popular for centuries, both for pleasure and practical purposes. With the fabulous choice of inexpensive fabrics that are widely available today, sewing has not lost its appeal. All the ideas in this book are not only beautiful to look at and fun to make, but useful too. Be inspired to make soft furnishings for the home and lifestyle accessories for yourself. Many of the projects would make lovely gifts for family and friends—if you can bear to part with them!

Those who love fabric will probably have a glorious stash of fabrics and trimmings waiting to be dipped into and turned into innovative creations. Large quantities of materials are not required, so you may find inspiration for a favorite fabric you have been waiting to use. Most of the projects featured are quick to make—ideal for a novice and those with little spare time. All the essential sewing techniques you need are explained in detail at the beginning of the book and each project has concise instructions and step-by-step photographs to guide you.

Whether you are a complete beginner or are already a keen needleworker, you will soon be learning new skills or embarking on a new hobby such as patchwork or quilting. And, more importantly, you will have a collection of beautiful handmade items to add style and individuality to your home!

the basics

materials and equipment

Fabrics

Most of the projects in this book are made from cotton and linen, which are natural fibers that are easy to work with—ideal for beginners. Fabrics made from natural fibers are prone to shrink so it is advisable to wash fabrics before cutting patterns out.

Cotton There is an enormous range of printed cotton fabrics available to buy online or from fabric and craft stores. Many are produced for patchwork and quilting purposes and are complemented by coordinating plain colored cottons. Also consider cotton lace such as eyelet lace, which lend themselves to feminine gifts.

Linen This strong, natural fabric is available in different weights. Linen is expensive and creases easily, but feels luxurious.

Upholstery fabric These durable fabrics are used to make soft furnishings. They come in lots of finishes and printed patterns and are usually 54 inches (137 cm) wide.

Fleece and felt Fleece is also known as polar fleece. It has a combed nap which makes it warm and cosy. Iron fleece with a cool iron. Felt is a non-woven material—it is inexpensive and comes in a large range of colors. Fleece and felt don't fray so they are ideal to cut motifs from to add as decoration to your creations.

Interfacing Stiffen fabric with interfacing. Non-woven and woven varieties come in different weights to suit their purpose. They are sold in packs or by the yard. Press iron-on (fusible) interfacing or baste sew-in interfacing to the wrong side of the fabric.

Batting Layer batting between fabrics to pad them to make quilts. Cotton and eco-friendly bamboo batting is available although polyester batting is most commonly used. Batting comes in different weights.

Tear-away stabilizer Place this non-woven material under fabric to be machine embroidered. It adds body and supports the fabric. Gently tear away the excess stabilizer after stitching.

Notions

Most of the items mentioned here can be found in good department stores or specialty sewing shops. It's always a good idea to keep a collection of buttons, ribbons and other trimmings as you come across them – you will soon find a use for them!

Buttons Use buttons for decoration as well as practical purposes. There is a huge selection available. Flat buttons have flat backs with two or four holes. Shank buttons have a loop underneath to sew through. Self-cover buttons can be covered with your choice of fabric; they are simple to use and come in different sizes.

Ribbons Colorful ribbons come in all sorts of widths and finishes. They can be used purely for decoration, or for loops, bag drawstrings, and to create woven ribbon designs.

Zippers Use a zipper to close two edges of fabric temporarily such as on a cushion cover or a bag. Stitch the zipper in place with a zipper foot on a sewing machine.

Trimmings There is an exciting selection of trimmings available to finish your projects. Sew-on trimmings such as braid, piping, bead edging and bobble trim can neaten straight edges. Braid can be stitched on top close to both long edges, whereas you insert trimmings with a flat flange in a seam using a piping or zipper foot. Just a few beads hand sewn at random are a lovely finishing touch.

Threads Choose sewing thread to match the fabric color. It should be strong and durable, with some 'give' in it. General-purpose mercerized cotton thread is suitable for woven natural fiber fabrics. General-purpose polyester thread is good on woven synthetic and knitted fabrics. Use the sewing thread or a heavy polyester thread for topstitching and sewing buttons. Generally, for patchwork and quilting use a 50 mercerized cotton thread. For professional results, use a machine embroidery thread for decorative zigzag stitching. Use embroidery threads such as widely available stranded cotton for hand embroidery and decorative running stitches. (Note the skeins are made up of six strands which have to be separated for fine work).

D-rings D-rings are metal 'D' shaped rings used to secure straps and fastenings. They come in various sizes.

Bias binding This is a strip of bias-cut fabric with the edges pressed under for binding curved and straight edges. Buy bias binding by the yard or in packs. It comes in different widths, a range of colors and a limited range of patterns. You can make your own with a bias binding maker.

Piping cord Cover this inexpensive cord with bias strips of fabric to make your own piping. It comes in different thicknesses.

Hook-and-loop tape This is a two-part tape: one tape has a looped mesh surface and the other a hooked surface. The two layers interlock when pressed together. The tapes can be sewn on or applied with their self-adhesive backing. Use hook-and-loop tape to fix blinds to battens or to fasten bags.

Metal eyelets Metal eyelets are available in a few different sizes and have a nickel, gilt, or painted finish.

Most come in a kit with an application tool; however small eyelets can be applied with special pliers.

Press studs Fasten bags or cushion covers with two-part metal or transparent plastic press studs.

Bag handles Bag handles can be made of various materials such as plastic, wood, metal, and bamboo. Choose a style to suit the design and size of your bag. Using ready-made handles is a simple way to give a professional finish to a bag.

Equipment

Even if you are new to sewing, you will probably have some of the basic equipment needed to get started. Keep the tools together and use sharp tools only on fabric and their trimmings, otherwise they may become blunt and dirty. Work on a clean, well lit surface. Keep sharp tools beyond the reach of small children and pets.

Pattern-making papers Most sewing stores supply pattern-making paper. Durable paper, such as parcel paper, is also suitable as it comes in large sizes. Tracing paper is useful for making patterns you will need to see through—when positioning motifs for example.

Pattern-making tools Use a fine pen or mechanical pencil for accurate drawing. Draw straight lines against a ruler and create circles with a pair of compasses. Use a set square to make accurate angles when drawing on paper and fabric.

Measuring tools A plastic-coated or cloth tape measure is useful for measuring curves. Use a yard stick to draw long lengths and to measure fabric quantities. A transparent 12-inch (30 cm) ruler is a handy size for drawing patterns on paper and fabric and for checking measurements. A 6-inch (15 cm) long sewing gauge has a slider to set at different levels for marking hems, or seams and as a quilting guide.

Fabric-marking tools Draw on fabric with an erasable pen; the marks made will gradually fade away. Alternatively, use a water-soluble pen: The marks can be removed with water. Tailor's chalk comes in different colors, in wedge and pencil form. Marks will brush off, although a slight mark may remain. Test all methods of marking fabric on scrap fabric first.

Scissors Bent-handled dressmaking shears are comfortable and accurate to use for cutting fabric as the angle of the lower blade allows the fabric to lie flat. The shears are available in different lengths, so test before buying. A top-quality pair of shears is expensive but will last a lifetime. A small pair of sharp embroidery scissors is vital for snipping threads and seam allowances. Pinking shears cut a zigzag fray-resistant edge for neatening seams and to cut fabrics that are prone to fraying. Cut paper patterns with dedicated scissors.

Needles Needles for sewing machines come in different sizes with different shaped points. The lower the number, the finer the point. Sizes 9–14 (70–90) are the most commonly used. A sharp-point needle is the most versatile for woven fabrics. Stitch non-woven fabrics with a ballpoint needle. In hand sewing needles, the higher the number the shorter and finer the needle. Use crewel embroidery needles for embroidery, they have a large eye and are easy to thread. Mattress needles are very long and are ideal for sewing through cushions—you could use one to attach buttons for example.

Pins Dressmaking pins come in various thicknesses; household pins are the most versatile. Use lace or bridal pins on delicate fabrics as other pins may mark the surface. Colored glass-headed pins show up well on a large expanse of fabric. Quilting pins are extra long to push through the layers of a quilt. They have colorful shapely ends so are easy to see. Curved basting pins are curved safety pins. They are used to secure fabric layers together. Be careful that they do not leave noticeable holes in the fabric.

Bodkin This needle-like tool has a large eye and blunt tip. Fasten a bodkin to a drawstring to draw it through a channel or to the end of a fabric tube to turn it right side out.

Rouleau turner Also known as a tube turner, a rouleau turner can be used in place of a bodkin. A latch hook at one end is hooked onto the end of a drawstring or fabric to draw it through an enclosure.

Bias binding maker Thread a bias or straight strip of fabric through this neat gadget: It will turn under the edges which you then press with an iron to make a binding. The bias binding maker comes in a range of widths.

techniques

The same basic methods occur throughout this book, so read this section before embarking on any project and try out the techniques on scrap fabric before making the item. When following instructions, it is important to use imperial or metric measurements but not a combination of the two.

Keep a basic sewing workbox at hand for all the projects. This should include dressmaking shears, embroidery scissors, ruler, tape measure, dressmaker's pins, a selection of sewing threads, a bodkin, and erasable pen (or water-soluble pen or tailor's chalk).

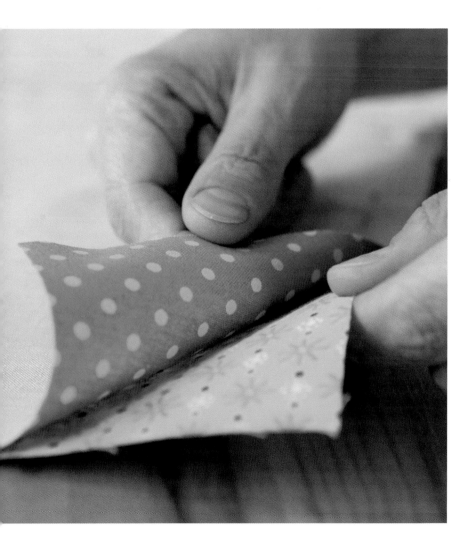

Cutting out

Most of the projects in this book are made from squares and rectangles and can be drawn directly onto the fabric using a ruler and an erasable pen (or water-soluble pen or tailor's chalk). There are also useful patterns and diagrams on pages 120–126.

Woven fabrics stretch differently if pulled in different directions. The grain is the direction in which the threads are woven. The lengthwise grain is called the warp and runs parallel with the selvedges. The warp has less stretch, which makes it easier to sew in this direction without the fabric stretching or puckering. The grain that runs across the fabric from selvedge to selvedge is the weft. It has a little more stretch than the warp. Cut rectangles and squares parallel with the warp and weft.

Most fabrics, especially printed ones, have a right and wrong side and in most cases it will be obvious which is the right side. Some fabrics, particularly plain woven ones, do not have a wrong side and are known as double-faced fabrics.

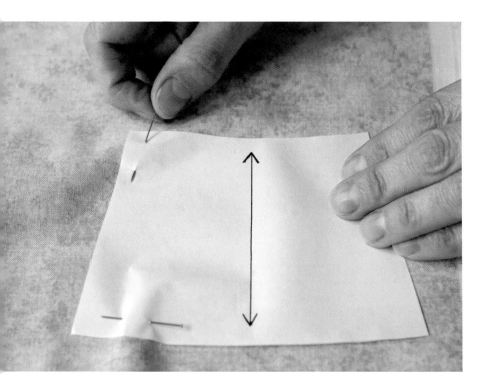

Using templates and patterns

Sewing patterns have an arrow on them which is the grain line. Keep the grain line parallel with the fabric selvedge when positioning the pattern. Lay the fabric smooth and flat on a table or the floor to cut it out. To cut pairs of patterns, fold the fabric lengthwise or widthwise to make a double layer. Pin the pattern or draw it on top. If the pattern has a fold line, match the fold line to the folded edge of the fabric. Pin the layers together and cut them out. Otherwise, keep the fabric in a single layer. Mark the position of any dots on the fabric with a pin, an erasable pen, or a water-soluble pen.

Positioning motifs

If your fabric has a distinctive motif, you may wish to show it whole, on the center of a cushion for example. Make a pattern on tracing or greaseproof paper so you can see through it. Fold the pattern into quarters to find the center, then open it out flat again. Mark the seam allowance and grain line. Lay the pattern over the motif on the fabric, matching grain lines and the center of the pattern to the center of the design. Pin in place and cut it out. You may need to buy a larger amount of fabric to allow for positioning motifs.

If the fabric has a repeat pattern, wide stripes, or checks, center these too so they will be positioned symmetrically when the item is made.

Stitching

Most of the projects in this book are worked using simple stitches on a sewing machine. Occasionally you will need to stitch by hand, when closing openings or basting.

Basting

Basting stitches join fabric layers together temporarily. The more you stitch and gain confidence, the less reliant on basting you will become. Baste by hand or use a long machine stitch. Basting is always useful for tricky areas such as joining many layers of fabric, stitching corners, or tight curves. Work basting stitches in a contrast colored thread so they are easy to see. Remove basting stitches once the seam has been completed.

Seams

Before stitching, match the seam allowances and pin together. Position pins at right angles to the seam line so you can stitch over them or insert the pins along the seam line and remove them as you stitch. Experiment and see which method you prefer—it could be a combination of both.

A flat seam is the most commonly used seam and occurs throughout these projects. With the right sides facing and raw edges of the seam allowance aligned, stitch the seam, keeping the same distance from the raw edges. Sewing machines have lines on the base plate that are standard seam allowance distances from the needle; keep the fabric's raw edges aligned with the relevant line to keep the size of the seam allowance constant. Stitch back and forth to start and finish a seam to stop the ends of the seam from unravelling.

Joining a curved edge to a straight edge is a little more difficult. To help the curve lay flat, snip into the curved seam allowance at regular intervals, then pin and stitch the seam (see right, above).

To topstitch on the right side, stitch parallel with a seam to emphasize it and to hold the seam allowance in place. Use contrasting or thick topstitching thread to accentuate the stitching.

Layering seams

Reduce the bulk of fabric in the seam allowance by trimming the fabric in the seam allowance by different amounts after the seam has been stitched (see right, below).

Neatening seams

Protect raw edges that will be prone to wear with a zigzag stitch.

Set the stitch width to about ⅛ inch (3 mm) wide and ⅛ inch (3 mm) apart. then stitch along the raw edges. Alternatively, trim the seam with a pair of pinking shears.

Clipping corners and curves

Use embroidery scissors to carefully snip 'V' shapes into curved seam allowances and across corners. This will help the fabric lay flat when it is turned through to the right side. Take care not to snip the stitching.

Slipstitching

Slipstitching is used to join two folded edges or one folded edge to a flat surface such as closing a gap in a seam or to secure binding.

Keep the stitches small. Working from right to left with a single thread, bring the needle out through one folded edge. Pick up a few threads on the opposite edge and insert the needle back through the folded edge about ¼-inch (6 mm) along from where it emerged. Repeat along the length.

Using bias strips

Strips cut on the bias can be used to make bias binding, piping, and rouleau. The bias is any direction on the fabric that is not the warp or weft. The bias will stretch so take care when stitching along the bias seams.

Cutting bias strips

Press the fabric diagonally at a 45-degree angle to the selvedge. This diagonal fold is the true bias. Press along the fold then open out flat. With an erasable pen, water-soluble pen, or tailor's chalk and ruler, draw lines the width of the bias strip parallel with the pressed line. To make bindings and piping, add 4 inches (10 cm) to the desired length for easing and turning under the ends. Add extra for joins.

Joining bias strips

Position one end of two strips at right angles with the right sides facing and matching the raw ends. Stitch the bias strips together taking a ¼-inch (6 mm) seam allowance. Press the seam open and cut off the extending corners.

Bindings

Although ready-made bias binding is widely available, it is economical and quick to make your own. Curved edges must be bound with bias binding; straight edges can be bound with bias or straight binding.

Create single bias or straight binding with a bias binding maker. The manufacturer's instructions will indicate the width to cut the binding.

Making bias binding

Push the strip (wrong side up) through the wide end of a bias binding maker. If necessary, poke a pin through the gap in the top of the bias binding maker to ease the binding through. The edges will be turned under as the binding emerges out of the narrow end. Press in place as you pull the binding through.

Attaching single binding

1 Open one folded edge of the binding. With right sides facing and matching the raw edges, pin the binding to the fabric. Stitch along the fold line.

2 Turn the binding to the underside, matching the pressed edge to the seam. Pin then slipstitch the pressed edge along the seam.

Attaching double binding

Make double binding from bias or straight strips. Press the strips lengthwise in half with wrong sides facing. Pin and stitch the binding to the fabric, matching the raw edges. Turn the binding to the underside. Pin then slipstitch the pressed edge along the seam or topstitch in place.

Piping

Piping gives a professional finish to cushions and other items. Ready-made piping comes in a limited range of colors and is costly, so make your own using inexpensive piping cord.

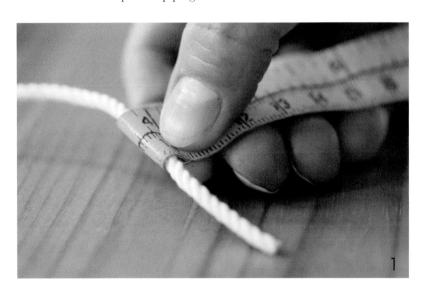

Making piping

1 Measure the circumference of the piping cord and add 1¼ inch (3 cm) for the seam allowances. Cut a bias strip of fabric in this width that is the length required plus 4 inches (10 cm) for ease and joining. Join bias strips if necessary.

2 Lay the cord along the center of the strip on the wrong side. Set the sewing machine to a long straight stitch for machine basting. Fold the strip lengthwise in half, enclosing the cord. Using a piping or zipper foot, stitch close to the piping cord.

Joining piping ends

1 To join the ends of piping neatly, allow a 1 inch (2.5 cm) overlap. Pin the piping in place to 2 inches (5 cm) on each side of the overlap. Unpick the piping basting for 2 inches (5 cm) on each side of the overlap to reveal the cord. Cut off 1 inch (2.5 cm) on half the strands at each end of the cord to thin it.

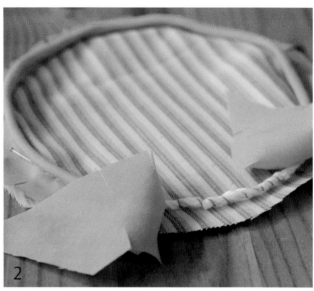

2 Twist the ends of the cord together and bind with thread. Make a few stitches to hold the cord together.

3 Wrap one end of the piping strip around the cord again. Turn under ¼ inch (6 mm) on the other end and wrap it around the cord. Baste the cord in place so it is ready for stitching.

Attaching piping

If the piping is to be stitched to a curved edge, snip the seam allowance at regular intervals so the seam allowance lays flat when applied to the curve. Pin the piping to the right side of the fabric, matching the raw edges. Snip the seam allowance at any corners. Baste in place by hand or machine using a piping or zipper foot.

Rouleau

A rouleau is a fine tube of bias cut fabric. It has many uses such as loops for fastening buttons, ties for fastening or purely for decoration. Being bias cut, the rouleau bends easily (see the lampshade on page 112).

1 Cut a bias strip of fabric. When calculating the size, double the required width and allow two ¼–⁵⁄₁₆ inch (6–7.5 mm) seam allowances. Add extra to the length for turning in ends or inserting inseams. Join bias strips if necessary. Fold lengthwise in- half with right sides facing. Stitch the long raw edges.

2 To turn right side out, fasten a bodkin to one end of the tube with a short length of thread. Ease the bodkin through the tube and it will pull the rouleau right side out. Alternatively, slip a rouleau turner into the tube, hook the end onto the end of the tube, and pull through. If the rouleau has wrinkled, steam it with an iron held just above the wrinkles.

the projects

eyelet lace pillow cover

This beautiful pillow cover is surprisingly simple to make. A layer of colored eyelet lace is applied over a contrasting colored fabric which shows through the cutwork shapes. If you cannot find a piece of colored eyelet lace, dye white cutwork cotton lace to achieve the effect.

you will need

- 16 inch (40 cm) square of pink cutwork cotton lace fabric

- ½ yard (40 cm) of 44-inch (112 cm) wide pale green plain cotton fabric

- matching sewing threads

- Four ¾-inch (2-cm) buttons

- 13¾ inch (35 cm) square pillow form

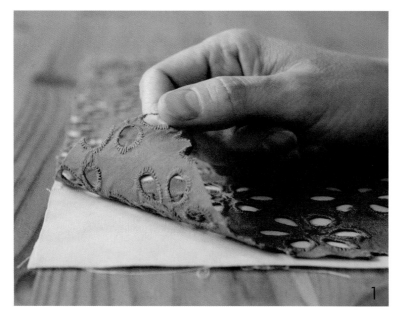

1 For the pillow cover front, cut a 15-inch (38 cm) square of eyelet lace and plain fabric. Pin the eyelet lace on top of the plain fabric with right sides facing up. Baste the outer edges together.

2 For the pillow cover backs, cut out two 15 x 10¾ inch (38 x 27.5 cm) rectangles of plain fabric. Press under ⅝ inch (1.5 cm) then 1¾ inches (4.5 cm) on one long edge of each back. Stitch close to the inner pressed edge to form a button stand. Using your sewing machine, stitch four buttonholes equally spaced along one button stand. Cut the buttonholes open.

3 With right sides facing up, overlap the back that has the buttonholes over the button stand on the other back by 2 inches (5 cm). Baste across the ends of the button stands.

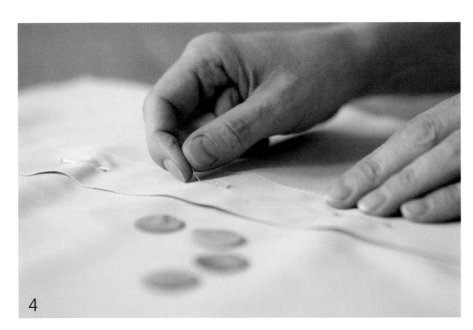

4 Mark the button positions at the center of the buttonholes with pins. Sew a button at each pin position on the underlying button stand.

5 With right sides facing, pin the front and back of the pillow cover together. Stitch the outer edges taking a ⅝ inch (1.5 cm) seam allowance. Clip the corners and turn the cushion right side out. Insert the pillow and fasten the buttons.

bolster pillow

Here is a classic bolster pillow brought up to date with a contemporary patterned cover with contrasting ends. Piping gives the cushion an elegant finish but can be omitted if you prefer.

you will need

- ⅔ yard (60 cm) of 44-inch (112 cm) wide blue with green patterned cotton fabric

- ⅓ yard (30 cm) of 44-inch (112 cm) wide lime green with turquoise patterned cotton fabric

- matching sewing threads

- 16-inch (40 cm) zipper

- 1⅓ yards (120 cm) of ⅛-inch (3 mm) diameter piping cord

- Bolster pillow form 18 x 6⅝ inches (45 x 17 cm)

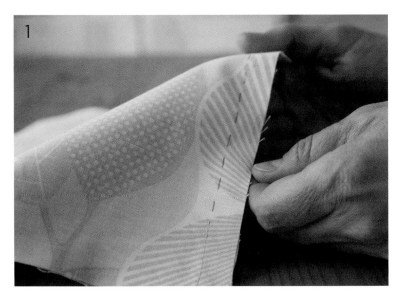

1 Cut a 22⅛ x 19-inch (56 x 48 cm) rectangle of pale blue with green patterned fabric. With right sides facing, fold the rectangle in half parallel with the short edges. Baste the short edges together taking a ⅝-inch (1.5 cm) seam allowance, forming a tube. Stitch for 1⅝ inches (4 cm) at each end of the basted seam. Do not remove the tacking. Press the seam open.

3 Using a zipper foot on the sewing machine, stitch the zip in place ¼ inch (6 mm) from the basted seam and across the ends of the zip. Take care not to sew through to the underside of the tube. Remove the basting and open the zip.

2 Place the zip centrally along the seam, face down. Pin and baste the zip in position (put your hand inside the tube to support the fabric and to help avoid sewing through to the underside of the tube). Turn the tube right side out.

4 Cut two 8-inch (20 cm) circles of lime green with turquoise patterned fabric. Cut 1⅝-inch (4 cm) wide bias strips measuring a total of 47¼ inches (120 cm) in length for the piping. Join the strips to make a continuous length, referring to the Joining Bias Strips technique on page 17.

5 Refer to pages 19–20 to make and attach piping to the circumference of the circles. Taking a ⅝-inch (1.5 cm) seam allowance, snip the seam allowance of the piping so it lays flat on the curves of the circles. Join the piping ends to make a neat ring of piping.

6 Fold the circles and ends of the tube into quarters, marking the edges of the fabric with a pin at each quarter mark. Snip the seam allowance of the tube at ⅜-inch (1 cm) intervals; this will help the seam allowance to lay flat. With right sides facing, pin the circles to each end of the tube, matching the quarter marks.

7 Using a zipper or piping foot on the sewing machine, baste and stitch the circles to the tube, taking a ⅝-inch (1.5 cm) seam allowance. Trim the seam allowances to layer them. Snip the curves and turn right side out. Insert the cushion pad and close the zip.

pyramid pillow

The unusual shape of this cushion is created with a few cleverly positioned seams, which are highlighted with a colorful bobble trim. Make the cushion from striped fabric to emphasize the shape.

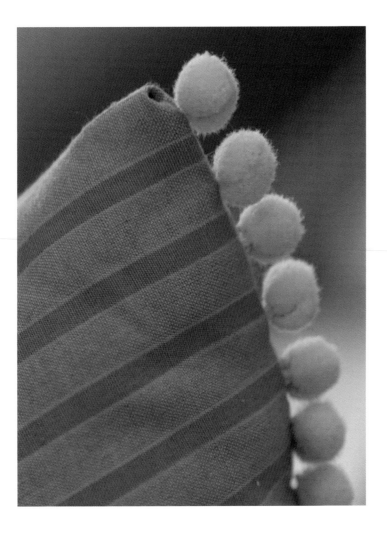

you will need

- ½ yard (50 cm) of 36-inch (90 cm) wide green and yellow striped cotton fabric

- matching sewing threads

- 1 yard (80 cm) of yellow pom-pom trim

- 14 ounces (400 g) of polyester toy filling

1 Cut a rectangle of striped fabric 32¾ x 17 inches (83 x 43 cm). Cut two 15¾-inch (40 cm) lengths of bobble trim. Pin and baste one length of pom-poms to one long edge of the rectangle between the center and ⅝ inch (1.5 cm) in from one short edge on the right side, allowing a ⅝-inch (1.5 cm) seam allowance.

2 With right sides facing, fold the rectangle in half parallel with the short edges. Pin the short and side basted edges together. Using a zipper or piping foot, stitch in place, taking a ⅝-inch (1.5 cm) seam allowance, leaving a 7-inch (18 cm) gap to turn through. Clip the corners then press the seam open.

3 Mark the center of the remaining pop-poms with a pin. Open out the raw edges of the cushion. Baste the trim to the raw edge on the right side, matching the pin to the seam, allowing a ⅝-inch (1.5 cm) seam allowance.

4 Fold the pillow at each end of the basted bobble trim, with right sides facing. Adjust the seam to lie across the center of the cushion, pin the raw edges together. Using a piping or zipper foot to accommodate the bobble trim, stitch in place, taking a ⅝-inch (1.5 cm) seam allowance. Clip the corners.

5 Turn the pillow right side out and fill firmly with the toy filling. Slipstitch the opening edges closed.

seat cushion

This chunky cushion is a comfortable addition to the house or garden. The softly padded edges are hand stitched and the center is buttoned with self-cover buttons to match the contrast colored sides of the cushion. The cushion is 16 inches (40 cm) square and has a practical carrying handle.

you will need

- ⅓ yard (30 cm) of 44-inch (112 cm) wide green dotted cotton fabric

- ¼ yard (10 cm) of 36-inch (90 cm) wide lightweight sew-in interfacing

- ½ yard (50 cm) of 44-inch (112 cm) wide pink with green spotted cotton fabric

- matching sewing threads, pink embroidery thread, button thread

- 14 ounces (400 g) toy filling

- quilting pins

- large crewel needle

- mattress needle

- Eight 1¼-inch (3 cm) self-cover buttons

1   Cut four 16¾ x 4¾-inch (42 x 12 cm) rectangles of green dotted cotton fabric for the gussets. Cut one 9½ x 3½-inch (24 x 9 cm) strip of green dotted cotton fabric and interfacing for the handle. Pin together. Fold the handle lengthwise in half with the right sides facing. Stitch the raw edges, taking a ⅜-inch (1 cm) seam allowance, leaving a 4-inch (10 cm) gap to turn through. Clip the corners.

2   Trim the seam allowance to layer it (see layering seams technique, page 15). Turn the handle right side out and press. Slipstitch the opening closed. Pin the handle centrally to the right side of one gusset. Stitch a 1-inch (2.5 cm) square at each end of the handle, stitch a cross shape across the square.

3   With right sides facing and taking a ⅜-inch (1 cm) seam allowance, pin and stitch two gussets together along the short edges, starting and finishing the stitching ⅜ inch (1 cm) from the long edges. Repeat to join all the gussets. Cut two 16¾-inch (42 cm) squares of pink with green spotted cotton fabric for the top and base.

4   With right sides facing and matching the gusset seams to the corners of the top cushion, pin and stitch the upper edges of the gussets to the cushion, pivoting the seams at the corners. Snip the corners and press the seams open. Repeat to stitch the base to the lower edges of the gussets, leaving 10 inches (25 cm) to turn through.

5 Turn the cushion right side out and fill firmly and evenly with toy filling. Slipstitch the opening closed. Fold the top of the cushion along one seam and pin the top and gusset together ¾ inch (2 cm) from the seam using quilting pins.

6 Thread a large crewel needle with a double length of embroidery thread. Knot the thread ends. Starting ¾ inch (2 cm) in from one corner, sew through both layers with a running stitch ¾ inch (2 cm) from the seams around the top of the cushion. Repeat on the base of the cushion.

7 Cover eight 1¼-inch (3 cm) self-cover buttons with green dotted fabric following the button manufacturer's instructions. Mark four button positions on the top and base of the cushion with pins 5 inches (12.5 cm) in from the side edges. Thread a mattress needle with a double length of button thread. Tie the thread ends to the shank of the button. Insert the needle through the cushion at the first button position and bring it out under the cushion at the corresponding position.

8 Cut off the needle. Thread one end of the thread through the shank of a button and tie it to the other thread, pulling the threads to dimple the cushion. Tie the threads securely together. Cut the thread ends under the button. Repeat to attach the other buttons.

tie-on cushion

Make relaxing in a sunny garden especially pleasant with a custom-made cushion to sit on. This cushion has ties at the back to fasten around the back struts of a chair. The cushion filling is anchored in place using a traditional tufting upholstery technique.

you will need

- pattern paper or parcel paper
- 1½-inch (4 cm) button
- approximately ⅔ yard (60 cm) of 44-inch (112 cm) wide pink striped cotton fabric
- matching sewing threads
- approximately 5 ounces (150 g) polyester toy filling
- ¾-inch (1.8 cm) bias binding maker
- 1 skein of pink stranded cotton embroidery thread
- mattress needle
- button thread
- Four ½-inch (1.2 cm) buttons

1 To make a pattern, draw a rectangle or square that is the size of the seat on pattern or parcel paper. Add 1 inch (2.5 cm) to the front and side edges. Draw around a 1½ inch (4 cm) button to round the corners. Add a ⁵⁄₁₆-inch (7.5 mm) seam allowance on all edges. Cut out the pattern. Use the pattern to cut two cushions from fabric.

2 Cut four 16 x 1⅜-inch (40 x 3.5 cm) bias strips of fabric for the ties. With right sides facing, fold and pin the ties lengthwise. Stitch the long edges, taking a ¼-inch (6 mm) seam allowance. Use a bodkin to turn the ties right side out. Turn in one end of each tie and slipstitch the ends closed.

3 Pin and baste the raw ends of the ties to the back edge of one cushion on the right side 1⅜ inches (3.5 cm) then 3⅜ inches (8.5cm) in from the side edges. With wrong sides facing, pin the cushions together.

4 Cut 1⅜-inch (3.5 cm) wide bias strips measuring the circumference of the cushion plus 4 inches (10 cm) in length for the binding. Join the strips if necessary and make a continuous length of bias binding using a ¾-inch (1.8 cm) bias binding maker, referring to the Joining Bias Strips and Making Bias Binding techniques on page 17.

5 Press under one end of the binding to start. Pin the binding to the cushion, taking a ⁵⁄₁₆-inch (7.5 mm) seam allowance. Stitch, leaving a 6-inch (15 cm) gap at the back. Ease the binding around the corners. Cut off the excess binding ⅝ inch (1.5 cm) beyond the start of the binding.

6 Stuff the cushion firmly. Pin, baste and stitch the gap closed, taking a ⁵⁄₁₆-inch (7.5 mm) seam allowance. Fold the binding over the edge of the cushion and slipstitch the pressed edge along the seam.

7 Cut embroidery thread into four 10-inch (25 cm) lengths. Cut the remaining thread into 1¾-inch (4.5 cm) lengths. Divide into four bunches and tie each bunch tightly around the center with a 10-inch (25 cm) length to make a tuft. Fold the tuft at the center, trim the thread ends level and cut the ties to the same length.

8 Mark four tuft positions on top of the cushion with pins. Thread a mattress needle with a double length of button thread. Insert the needle up through the underside of the cushion and out through the top at the first tuft position. Loop the thread around the center of one tuft and insert the needle back through the cushion.

9 Insert the needle through the hole of a button, insert the ends of the threads through the other buttonhole. Pull the threads tight to dimple the cushion, tie the thread ends securely together on top of the button. Cut off the excess thread. Repeat to attach the other buttons.

stationery folder

Keep paper, envelopes, or postcards in this smart stationery folder. As a finishing touch, choose a beautiful button to use as a feature for the loop fastening. The folder would also make a delightful place to store treasured letters.

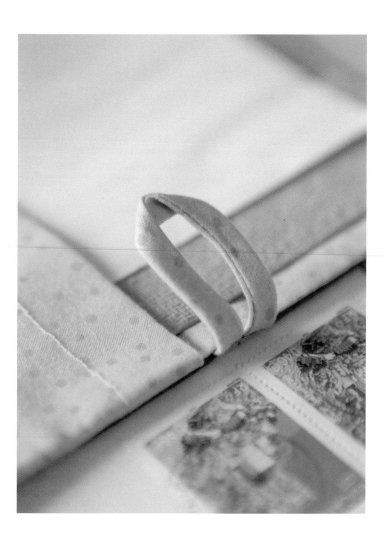

you will need

- ⅓ yard (30 cm) of 44-inch (112 cm) wide blue dotted cotton fabric

- ⅓ yard (30 cm) of 44-inch (112 cm) wide pink patterned cotton fabric

- matching sewing threads

- ⅓ yard (30 cm) of 36-inch (90 cm) wide stiff iron-on interfacing

- One 1¼-inch (3 cm) turquoise button

1 Use the template on page 120 to cut two pockets from blue dotted cotton fabric. Neaten the upper long edges of the pockets with a zigzag stitch. Press under ¾ inch (2 cm) on the upper edges. Stitch close to the zigzagged edges to hem the pockets.

2 Cut two 10⅝ x 7⅝-inch (27 x 19.5 cm) rectangles of both fabrics and interfacing. With right sides facing up, pin and baste the pockets to the lower section of the blue dotted rectangles which will be the linings, matching the raw edges. Fuse the interfacing to the wrong side of the pink patterned rectangles which will be the covers.

3 Cut an 4⅜ x 1¼-inch (11 x 3 cm) bias strip of blue dotted fabric for the button loop. Fold in half lengthwise with right sides facing. Stitch the long edges taking a ¼-inch (6 mm) seam allowance. Turn right side out with a bodkin to make a button loop. Baste the ends of the loop centrally to the right hand long edge of one cover on the right side, this will be the back.

4 With right sides facing, pin the covers on top of the linings. Taking a ⅝-inch (1.5 cm) seam allowance, stitch the raw edges, leaving the long left hand edge of the back cover and long right hand edge of the other cover open. Trim the seam allowance to layer it. Snip the corners. Turn right side out and press.

5 With the covers facing out and all edges level, pin the raw edges of the covers together. Cut a 10⅝ x 3⅞-inch (27 x 10 cm) bias strip of blue dotted fabric. Press the strip lengthwise in half to make a double bias binding.

6 Matching the raw edges, pin and baste the binding to the front cover with ⅝ inch (1.5 cm) extending at both ends. Stitch the binding to the folder taking a ⅝-inch (1.5 cm) seam allowance.

7 Pin under the ends of the binding. Fold the pressed edge of the binding to the back cover. Slipstitch along the seam. Sew a button to the front of the folder under the button loop.

ripple table runner

A table runner adds a touch of glamour to the dinner table. This colorful linen runner is shot through with sparkly metallic threads making it ideal for a party. The unusual ripple effect on the rows of tucks is easy to achieve. The runner measures 60 x 12 inches (150 x 30 cm). Buying the quantity of fabric listed below will provide enough fabric to make a set of matching napkins too.

you will need

- 2 yards (180 cm) of 54-inch (137 cm) wide metallic turquoise linen
- matching thread

1 Cut a 68½ x 13¾-inch (178 x 35 cm) rectangle of fabric for the runner. With wrong sides facing, press under 6¾ inches (17 cm) at one end of the runner. Stitch across the runner, ⅜ inch (1 cm) from the pressed edge to form the first tuck.

2 To form the next tuck, fold and press across the runner ¾ inch (2 cm) from the stitched line. Stitch across the runner, ⅜ inch (1 cm) from the pressed edge to form the second tuck. Repeat to stitch and press a total of five tucks. Repeat at the other end of the runner.

3 Press the tucks toward the center of the runner. Baste across the ends of the tucks. Stitch at right angles across the tucks 3⅜ inches (8.5 cm) in from (and parallel with) both long edges.

4 To hem the runner, press under ⅜ inch (1 cm) then ⅝ inch (1.5 cm) on the raw edges. Open out the fabric at the corners and cut diagonally across the allowance ¼ inch (6 mm) from the pressed corner.

5 Press under the diagonal edge. Refold the hem—the diagonally folded edges should meet edge to edge.

6 Slipstitch the mitered edges together. Stitch close to the inner edges of the entire hem.

7 Press the center of the tucks in the opposite direction towards the short edges of the runner.

bordered tablecloth

If you have never tried patchwork, this pretty tablecloth is an ideal first project as the contrasting border is joined with the simplest patchwork technique. The tablecloth measures 58 inches (150 cm) square.

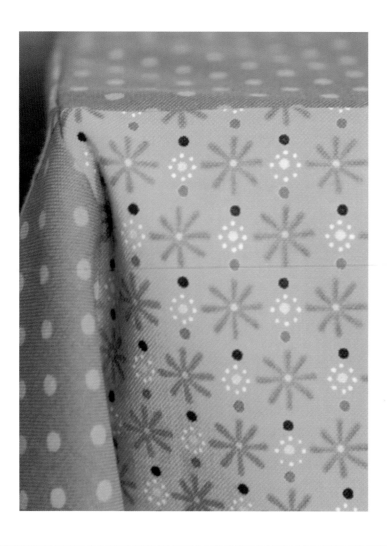

you will need

- 1¾ yards (140 cm) of 44-inch (112 cm) wide turquoise spotted cotton fabric

- 1¼ inch (110 cm) of 44-inch (112 cm) wide green floral cotton fabric

- matching sewing threads

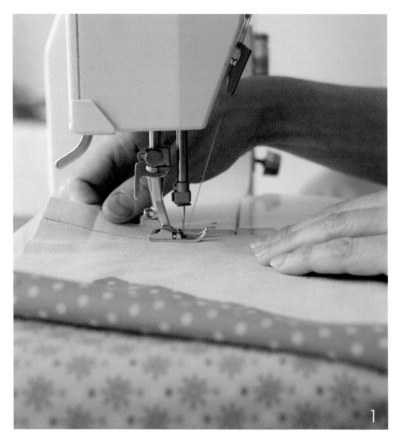

1 Cut one 42½-inch (108 cm) square and four 10⅜ inch (26.5 cm) squares of turquoise spotted fabric. Cut four 42½ x 10⅜-inch (108 x 26.5 cm) strips of green floral cotton fabric for the borders. With right sides facing, stitch a border strip to two opposite edges of the tablecloth taking a ⅝-inch (1.5 cm) seam allowance. Press the seams toward the borders. Neaten the seams with a zigzag stitch.

2 With right sides facing, stitch the small squares of tablecloth fabric to each end of the remaining border strips taking a ⅝-inch (1.5 cm) seam allowance. Press the seams toward the border then neaten the seams with a zigzag stitch.

3 With right sides facing, pin the border strips and small squares to the raw edges of the tablecloth, matching the seams. Insert a pin through the seams to match them. Stitch, taking a ⅝-inch (1.5 cm) seam allowance. Press the seams toward the border. Neaten the seams with a zigzag stitch.

4 To hem the tablecloth, press under ⅜ inch (1 cm) then ⅝ inch (1.5 cm) on the raw edges. Open out the fabric at the corners and cut diagonally across the allowance ¼ inch (6 mm) from the pressed corner.

5 Press under the diagonal edge for ¼ inch (6 mm). Refold the hem—the diagonally folded edges should meet edge to edge.

6 Slipstitch the mitered edges together. Stitch close to the inner edges of the entire hem.

bound napkin

Use this neat binding technique to finish the edges of napkins, tablecloths, runners, and throws. Make a smart set of napkins to coordinate with a tablecloth or match the border to the color scheme of your china.

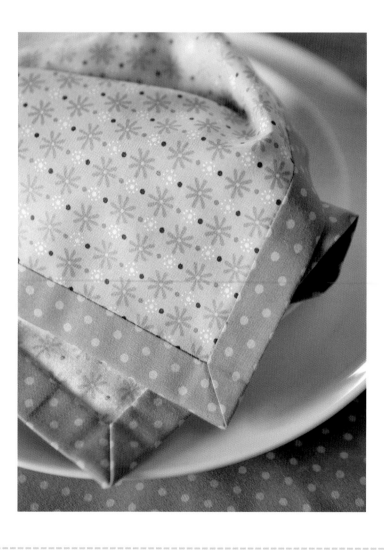

you will need

- ¼ yard (20 cm) of 44-inch (112 cm) wide turquoise spotted cotton fabric (for the binding)

- 15¾-inch (40 cm) square of green floral cotton fabric (for the napkin)

- matching sewing threads

1 Cut two 32¾-inch (82 cm) straight strips of 3 inch (8 cm) wide turquoise spotted fabric for the binding. With right sides facing, join the lengths, taking a ¼-inch (6 mm) seam allowance to make a continuous length. Press the seam open. Press the binding lengthwise in half. Open out the binding and press the long edges to meet at the center.

2 Open out the binding at one end and press under ¼ inch (6 mm). With the right sides facing and starting halfway along one edge of the napkin, pin and stitch the binding to the napkin, taking a ¾-inch (2 cm) seam allowance. Stitch along the fold line, finishing ¾ inch (2 cm) from the adjacent edge.

3 With wrong sides facing, fold the binding at a 45° angle from the corner. Next, fold the binding level with the stitched raw edges to lie along the adjacent edge of the napkin.

4 Mark the end of the previous stitching with a pin and stitch from this mark, finishing ¾ inch (2 cm) from the next adjacent edge. Continue all the way around the napkin, overlapping the pressed end of the binding.

5 Press the binding outwards from the napkin then turn it to the underside along the center fold line.

6 Pin the binding to the underside, folding under the fullness at the corners in a neat mitre. Slipstitch the pressed edges along the seams.

pocketed napkin

Make a set of pocketed napkins for a special occasion. The napkin edges are neatened with a wide zigzag stitch using a glossy machine embroidery thread. Trim the pocket with a pretty party decoration, a bead, or a button and slip a small gift or greeting card inside.

you will need

- ½ yard (40 cm) of 54-inch (137 cm) wide metallic turquoise linen

- matching machine embroidery threads

- One 7-inch (18 cm) square of soft iron-on interfacing

- tracing paper and pencil

- ruler

- ¼ yard (20 cm) of 12-inch (30 cm) wide tear-away stabilizer

- party decoration or large bead or button

1 Cut a 7-inch (18 cm) square of fabric. Fuse the interfacing to the fabric square. Use the template on page 121 to cut the pocket from tracing paper. Pin the template on the fabric matching the outer straight edges to two adjacent fabric edges. Draw around the curves with an erasable fabric pen. Use a straight stitch to stitch along the curved line with machine embroidery thread.

2 Set the sewing machine to a close zigzag stitch at the widest stitch width. Stitch along the curved line, with the straight stitching centered. To turn the stitching at the corners, keep the needle inserted at the inside edge of a corner, lift the presser foot and pivot the fabric. Continue stitching the pocket.

3 Carefully trim away the excess fabric outside the curved zigzag stitched line with a pair of sharp embroidery scissors. Draw the inner straight lines on the right side of the pocket with an erasable fabric pen and ruler.

4 Cut a 16-inch (40 cm) square of fabric for the napkin. Using an air-erasable fabric pen and ruler, draw a 1-inch (2.5 cm) margin inside the edges of the napkin. Pin the pocket to one corner of the napkin, matching the raw edges.

5 Cut four 16 x 1½-inch (40 x 4 cm) strips of tear-away stabilizer. Pin a strip of the stabilizer under each edge of the napkin. Set the sewing machine to a straight stitch. On the right sides, stitch along the straight drawn lines.

6 Set the sewing machine to a close zigzag stitch at the widest stitch width. Stitch along the straight lines with the straight stitching centered. To turn the stitching at the corners, keep the needle inserted at the outside edge of a corner, lift the presser foot and pivot the fabric. Continue stitching the napkin edges. To finish, overlap the zigzag stitching by ⅜ inch (1 cm).

7 Leave the trailing ends of thread. Pull the threads to the wrong side, thread them through a needle and work the threads through the back of the zigzag stitching for about 1¼ inches (3 cm). Cut off the excess threads. Gently pull away the tear-away stabilizer on each side of the zigzag stitching.

8 Carefully trim away the excess fabric outside the zigzag stitching with a pair of sharp embroidery scissors. Sew a party decoration or large bead to the pocket.

TIP Test the zigzag stitching on a scrap of fabric with a piece of tear-away stabilizer underneath before embarking on the napkin.

place mat

This pretty place mat measures a generous 15¾ x 12 inches
(40 x 30 cm). A layer of curtain interlining inside provides
added protection to the surface underneath and will
slightly cushion the plates and bowls you put on top.

you will need

- ½ yard (40 cm) of 54-inch
  (137 cm) wide pale blue linen

- ½ yard (40 cm) of 44-inch
  (112 cm) wide turquoise striped
  cotton fabric

- 27½ inches (70 cm) of ⅜-inch
  (1 cm) wide turquoise spotted
  ribbon

- matching sewing threads

- ½ yard (40 cm) of 54-inch
  (137 cm) wide curtain
  interlining

1 Cut a 13¼ x 10¾-inch (33 x 27 cm) rectangle of pale blue linen and two 13¼ x 4⅜-inch (33 x 11 cm) rectangles of turquoise striped fabric. With right sides facing, stitch the pale blue linen rectangle between the striped rectangles along the long edges, taking a ⅝-inch (1.5 cm) seam allowance. Press the seams open.

2 Cut two 13¼-inch (33 cm) lengths of spotted ribbon. On the right side, center each length over a seam and pin in place. Stitch close to the edges of the ribbons.

3 Cut a 17 x 13¼-inch (43 x 33 cm) rectangle of curtain interlining and pale blue linen. Lay the interlining out flat. Place the stitched place mat right side up on top, smooth the fabric outwards. Pin the pale blue rectangle on top with right sides facing.

4 Stitch the outer edges, taking a ⅝-inch (1.5 cm) seam allowance and leaving a 6 inch (15 cm) gap to turn through. Clip the corners then carefully trim the interlining close to the seam. Turn the place mat right side out. Press the edges. Slipstitch the gap closed.

bordered throw

Transform an inexpensive chenille throw by adding a deep border of patterned fabric. The throw has neat mitered corners and measures approximately 67 x 53 inches (170 x 135 cm). Alternatively, use a piece of chenille or woollen fabric to make the throw.

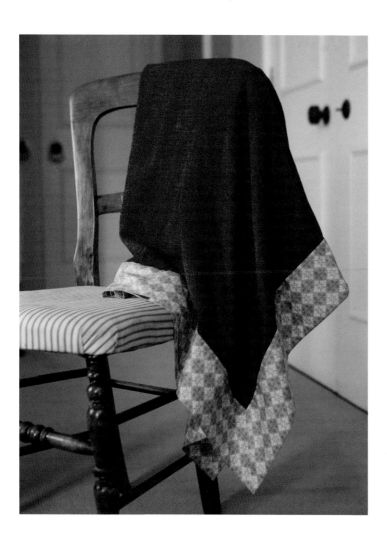

you will need

- chenille throw or rectangle of chenille fabric at least 54 x 40 inches (137 x 102 cm)

- 1⅔ yards (160 cm) of pink patterned cotton fabric

- matching sewing threads

1 Cut a rectangle of chenille 52⅜ x 38⅜ inches (133 x 98 cm). Cut two strips of pink patterned cotton fabric for the border. Refer to the diagram on page 122 to cut the ends of the borders to points. Press under ⅝ inch (1.5 cm) on one long edge of each border.

2 With right sides facing and matching the pressed edges, stitch the short borders between the long borders at the mitered ends, finishing ⅝ inch (1.5 cm) from the long raw edges. Clip the corners. Press the seams open, using a moistened finger to finger-press inside the corner where the iron will not reach.

3 With right sides facing, pin and stitch the long raw edges of the border to the throw taking a ⅝-inch (1.5 cm) seam allowance and pivoting the seam at the corners. Press the seam toward the border. Trim the seam allowance on the rectangle to ⅜ inch (1 cm) to layer the seam.

4 Pin the pressed edges of the border along the seam. Press the border in half. Slipstitch the pressed edge along the seam.

patchwork play mat

Here is a fun project which would be a delightful gift for a young child. The softly padded play mat is made up of patchwork squares and is an ideal introductory patchwork project. The play mat measures 41½ inches (105 cm) square and is tied with felt starfish.

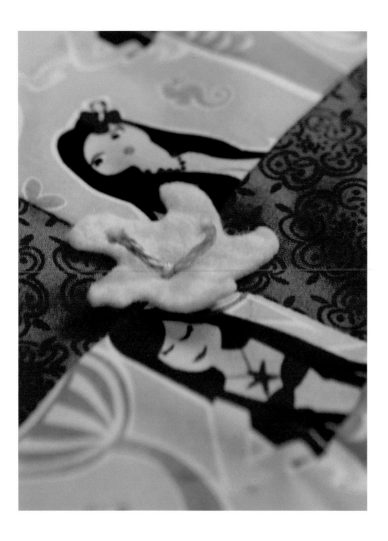

you will need

- ¾ yard (70 cm) of 44-inch (112 cm) wide turquoise patterned cotton fabric

- 2½ yards (220 cm) of 44-inch (112 cm) wide pink patterned cotton fabric

- matching sewing threads

- 1¼ yards (110 cm) of 45-inch (114 cm) wide 4 ounce (113 g) batting

- curved basting pins (optional)

- 2-inch (5 cm) bias binding maker

- 9-inch (23 cm) square of yellow felt

- large-eyed needle

- turquoise 3-ply cotton embroidery thread

1 Cut thirteen 8⅝-inch (22 cm) squares of turquoise patterned fabric and twelve squares of pink patterned cotton fabric. Arrange the squares in five rows of five squares, alternating the colors. With right sides facing and taking a ⅜-inch (1 cm) seam allowance, stitch each row together.

2 Press the seams of the first row in the same direction, the seams of the next row in the opposite direction and so on. With right sides facing and taking a ⅜-inch (1 cm) seam allowance, stitch the first and second row together, matching seams. Stitch the remaining rows to form a square. Press the seams downwards.

3 Lay a 44-inch (112 cm) square of pink patterned fabric flat, wrong side up. This will be the backing fabric. Place the batting on top. Center the patchwork on top, smooth the layers outwards from the center. Baste or pin together with curved basting pins. Baste the outer edges together.

4 Cut the backing fabric and batting ⅜ inch (1 cm) larger all around than the patchwork. Cut two 40⅞ x 3¾-inch (104 x 9.5 cm) and two 42⅛ x 3¾-inch (107 x 9.5 cm) strips of pink fabric for the binding. Make the binding using a 2-inch (5 cm) bias binding maker (see page 17).

5 Stitch the shorter bindings to the side edges of the play mat (see attaching bias bindings technique, page 18), taking a ¾-inch (2 cm) seam allowance.

6 Fold and pin the binding over the edge of the play mat. Slipstitch the pressed edge of the bindings along the seams.

7 With ⅝ inch (1.5 cm) extra at each end, stitch the remaining bindings to the raw edges. Fold and pin the binding over the edge of the play mat, turning in the ends to start and finish. Slipstitch the pressed edges along the seams.

8 Use the template on page 122 to cut 16 starfish shapes from yellow felt. Pin a starfish on each inner corner of the patchwork squares. Thread a large-eyed needle with a length of embroidery thread. Insert the needle through the center of one starfish, through all the layers, leaving a trailing length of thread. Bring the needle to the right side close to where it emerged.

9 Tie the embroidery threads tightly together with a double knot. Trim the thread ends ⅝ inch (1.5 cm) above the knot. Repeat on each starfish. Remove the tacking or basting pins.

TIP Remember to buy a larger amount of fabric if you wish to center motifs on the patchwork squares (see the Positioning Motifs Technique, page 14).

potpourri sachet

Freshen your wardrobe with an elegant sachet of fragrant lavender. Make the sachet from a fine, loosely woven fabric to allow the scent to escape. As a finishing touch, trim the sachet with a velvet ribbon and button.

you will need

- ¼ yard (20 cm) of 36-inch (90 cm) wide loosely woven lightweight cotton or linen pale turquoise fabric

- matching sewing threads

- pale turquoise stranded cotton embroidery thread

- crewel embroidery needle

- 2 handfuls of dried lavender

- ⅓ yard (30 cm) of ¼-inch (6 mm) wide green velvet ribbon

- One ¾-inch (2 cm) pale turquoise button

1 Cut two 6-inch (15 cm) squares of loosely woven lightweight cotton or linen pale turquoise fabric. With right sides facing and taking a ⅜-inch (1 cm) seam allowance, stitch the outer edges leaving a 2⅝-inch (6.5 cm) opening centrally along one edge to turn right side out.

2 Trim the seam allowance to ¼ inch (6 mm) and snip the corners. Turn the square right side out and press.

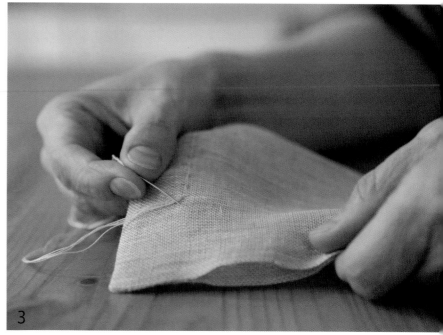

3 Using four strands of cotton embroidery thread, sew a 1-inch (2.5 cm) deep border on the square with a running stitch, leaving a gap to match the gap on the outer edge. Do not remove the needle and thread.

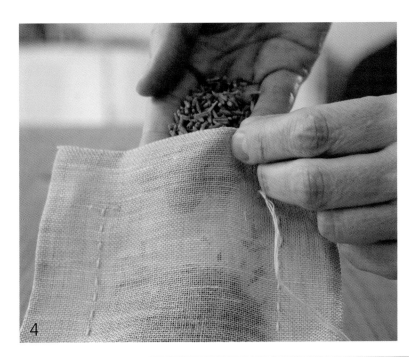

4 Fill the inner square with dried lavender. Finish the running stitch to close the gap and enclose the lavender. Slipstitch the gap on the outer edge closed.

5 Bend the ribbon into a loop. Overlap the ribbon 1¾ inches (4.5 cm) from the ends. Sew securely to the top corner of the inner square as a hanging loop. Sew a button on top. Cut the ends of the ribbon diagonally to prevent fraying.

clothes caddy

Make a fabric envelope to store delicate clothing. This envelope makes a delightful gift, especially when it is enhanced with a pretty flower brooch. The flower petals are made using a rouleau and have a button center. The brooch is pinned to the flap of the envelope and can be removed to wear.

you will need

- ½ yard (50 cm) of 44-inch (112 cm) wide pink plain cotton fabric

- ⅓ yard (30 cm) of 44-inch (112 cm) wide pale green patterned cotton fabric

- matching sewing threads

- ½ yard (40 cm) of 36-inch (90 cm) wide medium sew-on interfacing

- ¾-inch (1.8 cm) press stud

- ⅓ yard (30 cm) of 44-inch (112 cm) wide pale green plain cotton fabric

- ¾-inch (2 cm) pale green plain button

- ¾-inch (2 cm) brooch pin

1 Cut one 24¾ x 5¼-inch (63 x 13 cm) rectangle of plain pink fabric, two of pale green patterned fabric and three of interfacing. Baste the interfacing to the wrong side of the fabric pieces.

2 With right sides facing, pin and stitch the plain fabric between the patterned fabric rectangles along the long edges, taking a ⅝-inch (1.5 cm) seam allowance. Trim the interfacing in the seam allowance. Press the seams open.

3 Cut one 24¾ x 13¼-inch (63 x 33 cm) rectangle of plain pink fabric for the lining. With right sides facing, pin and stitch the lining to the envelope taking a ⅝-inch (1.5 cm) seam allowance, leaving a gap to turn along one short edge. Trim the seam allowance to layer the seam. Snip the corners and turn right side out.

4 Press the lining to the inside. Slipstitch the opening closed. With the right side outside, press over 6 inches (15 cm) at one end of the envelope for the flap. Open the flap out flat. Press over 8 inches (20 cm) at the other end to form the envelope. Baste close to the side edges. Topstitch close to the side edges then ⁵⁄₁₆ inch (7.5 mm) inside the side edges.

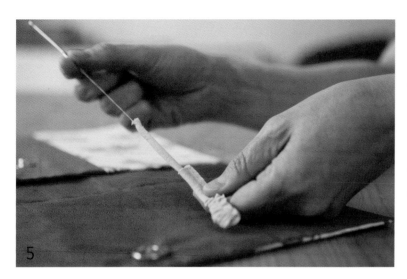

5 Sew a press-stud under the flap. Sew the corresponding press-stud to the front of the envelope, slip some clothing into the envelope to help judge the positioning. Cut a 11⅞ x 1-inch (30 x 2.5 cm) bias strip of pale green plain fabric. Fold lengthwise in half with right sides facing. Stitch the long edges taking a ¼-inch (6 mm) seam allowance. Turn right side out with a bodkin to make a rouleau.

6 The rouleau will have stretched so trim the ends so it is 12 inches (30 cm) long. Divide the rouleau into five 2⅜-inch (6 cm) sections, mark each division with a pin. Anchor a double length of thread to one end. Fold each section into a loop for a petal, matching the pins to the ends of the rouleau at the center of the 'flower'. Stitch through the folds and remove the pins.

7 Join the ends securely at the center. Sew a button to the center of the flower. Sew a brooch pin to the back of the flower. Pin the flower to the flap of the envelope.

tissue case

This beautiful case is made for a small box of tissues. It's quick to make and is an ideal get-well-soon gift for a special friend. It would look equally good in a bathroom or guest bedroom. A row of coordinating buttons is a neat finishing detail.

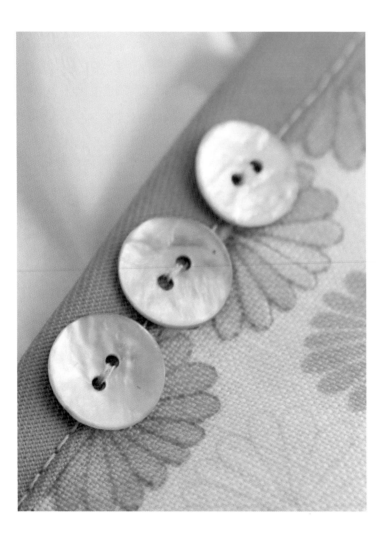

you will need

- 14-inch (35 cm) square of plain turquoise fabric
- ⅓ yard (30 cm) of 44-inch (112 cm) wide patterned turquoise and green fabric
- matching sewing threads
- Three ½-inch (1.2 cm) green buttons

1 Cut two 11⅜ x 2⅜-inch (29 x 6 cm) bias strips of plain fabric. Press the strips lengthwise in half with wrong sides facing to make a double bias binding. Cut a 12⅝ x 11⅜-inch (32 x 29 cm) rectangle of patterned fabric. Using a zigzag stitch, stitch the long raw edges to neaten them.

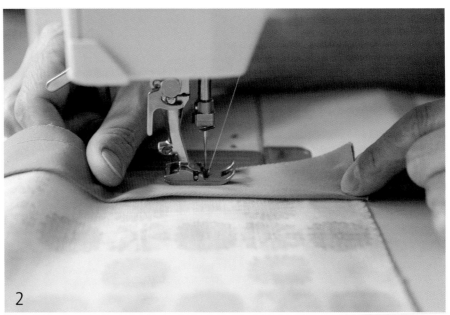

2 Taking a ⁵⁄₁₆-inch (7.5 mm) seam allowance, stitch one binding to the wrong side of one short edge of the rectangle. Repeat on the other short edge.

3 Press the seams towards the binding. Fold the binding over the seam allowance and pin the pressed edge along the stitching on the right side. Topstitch close to the inner pressed edges.

4 With right sides facing, fold the bound edges to meet at the center of the long edges. Stitch the raw edges, taking a ⅝-inch (1.5 cm) seam allowance, stitch back and forth a few times over the ends of the binding to reinforce the seam.

5 Open the case and lay one seam out flat at one corner. Fold one end of the seam allowance to form a triangle. Stitch across the raw edge of the triangle to form a dart. Repeat at each corner.

6 Turn the tissue case right side out. Slip a pile of tissues inside. Sew three buttons in a row along the seam of one binding.

drawstring bag

Ribbon weaving is a great way to use up scraps of ribbon and add interest and texture to this otherwise traditional drawstring bag. Choose ribbons to match the fabric of the bag, then add a contrast color too—such as the turquoise on this pink and cream bag.

you will need

- ¼ yard (20 cm) of 36-inch (90 cm) wide lightweight iron-on interfacing

- ¼ yard (20 cm) of 36-inch (90 cm) wide lightweight cream fabric

- 3¾ yards (340 cm) of ⅞-inch (2.2 cm) wide cream ribbon

- 1⅝ yards (140 cm) of 1-inch (2.4 cm) wide turquoise ribbon

- ⅔ yard (60 cm) of ¹¹/₁₆-inch (1.8 cm) wide cream spotted ribbon

- 2½ yards (220 cm) of 1-inch (2.4 cm) wide pink petersham ribbon

- ½ yard (40 cm) of 54-inch (137 cm) wide pink with cream soft upholstery fabric

- matching sewing threads

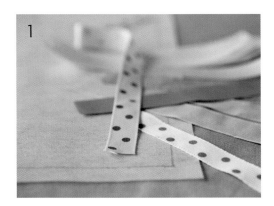

1 Cut one 14⅜ x 6⅞-inch (36.5 x 17.5 cm) rectangle of lightweight iron-on interfacing and lightweight cream cotton fabric. Lay the interfacing glue side up on the ironing board. Draw a ⅝-inch (1.5 cm) seam allowance within the outer edges with a water-soluble pen. For the warp (vertical) ribbons, cut eight 6⅞-inch (17.5 cm) lengths of cream ribbon, four 6⅞-inch (17.5 cm) lengths of turquoise ribbon and three 6⅞-inch (17.5 cm) lengths of cream spotted ribbon.

2 Place one cream ribbon ⅝-inch (1.5 cm) in from one short edge. Pin at the upper edge. Next, pin a turquoise ribbon, a cream ribbon then a cream spotted ribbon. Repeat this sequence twice then pin a cream ribbon, a turquoise ribbon and a cream ribbon.

3 Cut six 14⅜-inch (36.5 cm) lengths of pink petersham ribbon for the weft (horizontal) ribbons. Weave the weft ribbons in and out of the pinned ribbons. Pin the ribbons at the ends, keep the woven area within the drawn seam allowance.

4 With a moderate dry iron, press the ends of the ribbons to fuse them to the interfacing. Press the entire surface of the weaving, gradually removing the pins as you iron. Turn the weaving over and iron the wrong side. Baste the weaving right side up on the lightweight cream fabric rectangle.

5

5 Cut two 15 x 14⅜-inch (38 x 36.5 cm) rectangles of pink soft furnishing fabric for the bag. With right sides facing, pin and stitch the weaving between one short edge of each side of the bag taking a ⅝-inch (1.5 cm) seam allowance. Neaten the seams with a zigzag stitch. Press the seams towards the bag sides. Topstitch the sides close to the seams.

6

6 Cut two 13-inch (33 cm) lengths of turquoise ribbon for the channels. Press under ¼ inch (6 mm) twice on each end. Hand stitch the ends in place. With right sides facing up, pin the channels centrally 4½ inches (11.5 cm) below the upper short edges of the bags. Stitch close to both long edges of the channels.

7

8

7 Fold the bag in half with right sides facing and matching the weaving seams. Pin and stitch the side edges taking a ⅝-inch (1.5 cm) seam allowance. Snip the corners then press the seams open. Neaten the seams with a zigzag stitch.

8 Press under ⅜ inch (1 cm) then press 1½ inches (4 cm) to the inside at the upper edge. Stitch close to the inner pressed edge to hem the bag. Cut the remaining cream ribbon in half. Using a bodkin, thread one length through the channels. Knot the ends together. Trim the ribbon ends diagonally. Repeat with other ribbon, starting at the other end of the channels.

market bag

This small, chic, and practical shopping bag has useful pockets on the sides for extra storage. It has ready-made handles which are available from sewing or craft shops. They give a highly professional finish to handmade bags. The bag measures 15¾ x 12 inches (40 x 30 cm), excluding the handles.

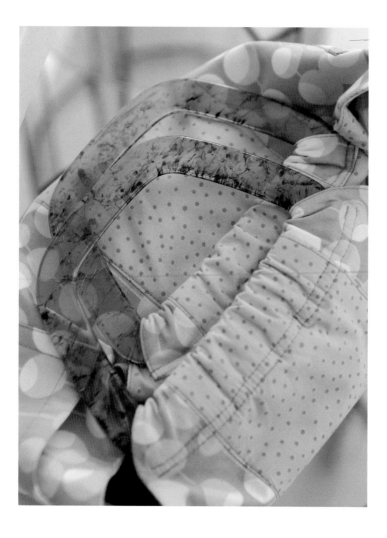

you will need

- ½ yard (40 cm) of 44-inch (112 cm) wide green patterned cotton fabric

- 1 yard (80 cm) of 44-inch (112 cm) wide green dotted cotton fabric

- matching sewing threads

- 1 yard (80 cm) of 36-inch (90 cm) wide medium sew-in interfacing

- Two 6½-inch (16.5 cm) D-shaped amber plastic bag handles

1 Use the template on page 123 to cut two shopping bags to the fold from both fabrics and interfacing. Cut two 8 x 7½-inch (20.5 x 19 cm) rectangles of green patterned fabric and interfacing for the pockets. Baste the interfacing to the wrong side of the green patterned fabric pieces.

2 Press under ⅜ inch (1 cm) then ⅝ inch (1.5 cm) on the upper short edges of the pockets. Stitch close to both edges to hem the pockets. Press under ⅝ inch (1.5 cm) on the raw edges of the pockets.

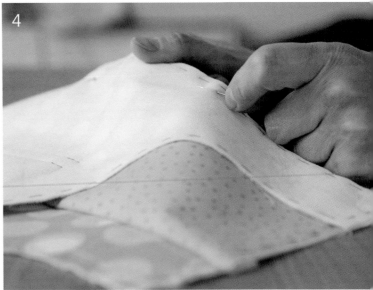

3 With right sides facing up, pin each pocket centrally to a bag with the short lower edge 1¾ inches (4.5 cm) above the lower edge of the bags. Topstitch close to the side and lower edges of the pockets. Stitch again ¼ inch (6 mm) inside the first stitching. Cut four 14½ x 5½-inch (37 x 14 cm) rectangles of green dotted fabric and two of interfacing for the bands.

4 Tack the interfacing to the wrong side of two bands. With right sides facing, pin and stitch the bands between the bags along the long straight edges taking a ⅝-inch (1.5 cm) seam allowance. Trim the interfacing in the seam allowances and press the seams toward the bands. Topstitch the bands close to the seams.

5 With right sides facing, fold the bags along the fold lines, matching the seams at the lower edges. Stitch the lower edge taking a ⅝-inch (1.5 cm) seam allowance. Trim the interfacing in the seam allowance and press the seam open.

6 Follow steps 4–5 to make the lining from the green dotted fabric pieces, omitting the interfacing and topstitching. Turn the lining right side out. Slip the lining in the bag with right sides facing, matching the raw edges. Pin and stitch the curved edges together taking a ¼-inch (6 mm) seam allowance. Clip the curves.

7 Turn the bag right side out by pulling the lining through the short upper edges. Press the lining inside the bag. Baste the lining and bag together 3½ inches (9 cm) below the upper raw edges. Topstitch the bag close to the curved edges. Press and baste under ⅜ inch (1 cm) on the upper raw edges.

8 Slip one upper edge through one bag handle. Pin the pressed edge to match the inner tacked line, forming a channel enclosing the handle. Baste, then stitch close to the pressed edge, laying the channel flat a section at a time to stitch in place. Stitch again 5⁄16 inch (7.5 mm) inside the pressed edge. Repeat to attach a bag handle to the other upper edge of the bag.

scalloped quilt

This vibrant reversible quilt measures 40 x 30 inches (100 x 75 cm), so it would make a super cozy gift for a little one. Choose a fabric that has stripes running parallel with the selvedges—this will help you keep the quilting lines straight as you simply follow the line of the stripes.

you will need

- thin card
- pen and ruler
- pattern paper or brown parcel paper
- 1¼ yards (110 cm) of 44-inch (112 cm) wide cotton pink striped fabric
- 1¼ yards (110 cm) of 44-inch (112 cm) wide cotton blue checkered fabric
- 1¼ yards (110 cm) of 36-inch (90 cm) wide 2 ounce (56 g) batting
- matching sewing threads
- curved basting pins (optional)
- matching quilting thread

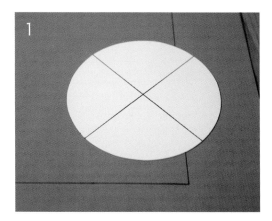

1 Cut a 5-inch (12.5 cm) diameter circle of thin card to use as a template for drawing the scallops. Divide the circle into quarters with a pen and ruler. To make a pattern, cut a 40 x 30-inch (100 x 75 cm) rectangle of pattern paper or brown parcel paper. Draw a 2½-inch (6.25 cm) deep margin inside the rectangle.

2 Place the circle template on one corner, matching the quarter lines to the inner corner of the margin. Draw around three-quarters of the circle on the margin. Repeat on each corner. Move the template along the inner edges of the margin and draw a row of semi-circles edge to edge for the scallops. Cut out the pattern along the scalloped edges.

3 Cut a 41½ x 31½-inch (104 x 79 cm) rectangle from both fabrics and batting. Lay the striped fabric out flat wrong side up, pin the pattern centrally on top. Draw around the scallops with an air-erasable fabric pen. Lay the checkered fabric right side up on the batting. Smooth the fabric outwards from the center.

4 With right sides facing, place the striped fabric on top of the checkered fabric and batting. Working outwards from the center, smooth the fabric outwards and baste or pin the layers together using curved basting pins.

5 Starting on the curve of one scallop, stitch along the drawn lines, leaving a 15-inch (37.5 cm) gap on one edge to turn right side out. Remove the basting pins.

6 On the right side of the checkered fabric, use the pattern to draw the unstitched scallops with an erasable fabric pen. Baste or re-pin the edges of the gap. Stitch along the drawn lines to secure the batting to the checkered fabric. Do not catch in the striped fabric. Continue stitching the scallops on the striped fabric but without stitching through the checkered fabric and batting.

7 Trim away the batting in the seam allowance close to the stitching. Trim the seam allowance to ¼ inch (6 mm). Carefully snip the curves and corners. Turn right side out and gently press the edges of the scallops. Turn the raw edges of the gap to the inside along the stitching and slipstitch the scallops together.

8 Baste the layers together or pin with curved basting pins. Lay the quilt out flat, striped side up. Thread the sewing machine with quilting thread. Starting at the center at the top of the quilt, stitch between the inner corners of the scallops, following the lines of the stripes with the sewing machine set to a long stitch length.

picnic blanket

There is always plenty to take on a picnic. This cozy picnic blanket makes life easy—as it can be folded in half, rolled up, and fastened with straps and D-rings. A handy wrist band keeps your hands free to carry that all-important picnic basket. The blanket measures 51 inches (130 cm) square.

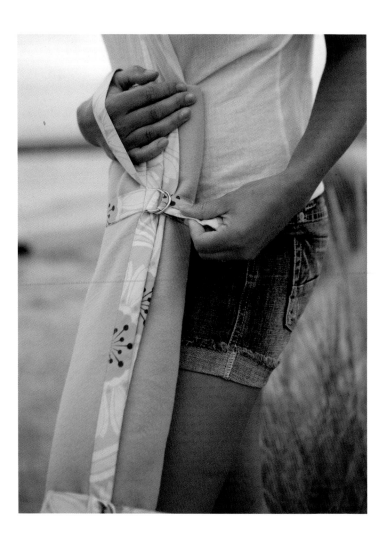

you will need

- 51-inch (130 cm) square of green fleece

- 12-inch (30 cm) diameter circle of paper or a plate

- 1¼ yards (1 m) of 44-inch (112 cm) wide green patterned fabric

- ¼ yard (20 cm) of 36-inch (90 cm) wide light sew-in interfacing

- Four 1-inch (2.5 cm) D-rings

- 2-inch (5 cm) bias binding maker

2 From patterned fabric and interfacing, cut two 17 x 2⅞-inch (43 x 7.5 cm) straight strips for the straps and one 15¾ x 2⅞-inch (40 x 7.5 cm) straight strip for the wrist band. Baste the interfacing to the wrong side of the fabric pieces. Press lengthwise in half with the wrong sides facing. Open out flat then press under ⅜-inch (1 cm) on the long edges.

1 To shape the rug, round off the corners of the fleece by placing a 12-inch (30 cm) diameter plate or circle on one corner. Draw around the circle between the adjacent side edges of the blanket with an erasable pen. Cut along the curve. Repeat on the other corners.

3 Press under ⅜ inch (1 cm) on one end of each strap. Refold in half. Topstitch close to the pressed edges of the straps and wrist band. Pin and baste the raw end of one strap to the blanket on one edge close to a curved corner. Baste the other strap to the rug 12⅜ inches (31.5 cm) from the first strap on the same edge of the rug. Fold the wrist band in half. Baste the raw ends to the blanket next to the second strap.

4 Cut two 2⅞-inch (7.5 cm) squares of patterned fabric and interfacing for the D-ring holders, baste the interfacing to the wrong side. Fold in half with right sides facing. Stitch the long edges, taking ⅜-inch (1 cm) seam allowances. Trim the seam allowances, turn right side out and press.

5 Slip two D-rings onto each D-ring holder. Pin the raw ends together and baste on top of the straps, matching the raw ends.

6 From patterned fabric, cut 3¾-inch (9.5 cm) wide bias strips measuring a total of 5½ yards (5 m) for the binding. Join the strips and make a continuous length of bias binding using a 2-inch (5 cm) bias binding maker (see page 17).

7 Press under one end of the binding to start. Refer to the Attaching Bias Binding technique on page 18 to bind the blanket, taking a ¾-inch (2 cm) seam allowance. Ease the binding around the corners. Cut off the excess binding ⅝ inch (1.5 cm) beyond the start of the binding.

8 Fold the binding over the edge of the blanket, and baste the pressed edge along the seam. Topstitch the binding close to the pressed edge.

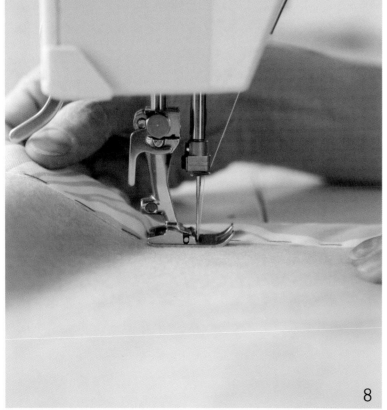

beach bag

Pack all you need for a fun day at the beach into this deep and roomy beach bag. Choose two contrasting fabrics that work well together; the bag has a distinctive band and shoulder strap that matches the lining. The bag measures 12½ inches (32 cm) wide x 15¾ inches (40 cm) high.

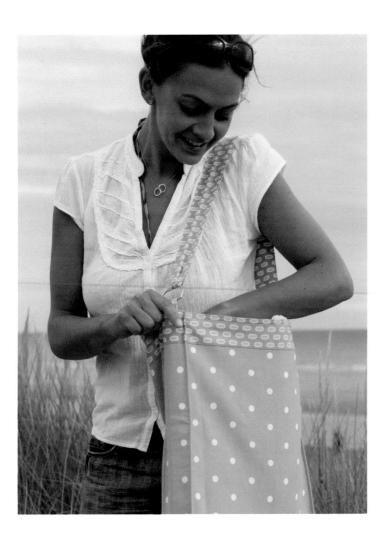

you will need

- ⅝ yard (50 cm) of 54-inch (137 cm) wide green spotted soft furnishing fabric

- ¾ yard (70 cm) of 36-inch (90 cm) wide medium sew-in interfacing

- ⅞ yard (80 cm) of 44-inch (112 cm) wide pink patterned cotton fabric

- matching sewing threads

- ⅓ yard (30 cm) of 36-inch (90 cm) wide light sew-in interfacing

- Two 2-inch (5 cm) D-rings

2 With right sides facing, pin and stitch the bands to the upper edges of the bag, taking a ⅝-inch (1.5 cm) seam allowance. Press the seams open. With right sides facing, pin and stitch the side edges of the bags, matching the band seams, taking a ⅝-inch (1.5 cm) seam allowance. Press the seams open.

1 Refer to the diagram on page 124 to cut two bags from green spotted fabric and medium sew-in interfacing. Cut two 16¾ x 3¼-inch (43 x 8 cm) bands of pink patterned fabric and medium sew-in interfacing. Baste the interfacing to the wrong side of the fabric pieces.

3 With right sides facing, pin and stitch the base of the bag, taking a ⅝-inch (1.5 cm) seam allowance. Press the seam open. With right sides facing, fold the lower ends of the side seams to match the ends of the base seam. Stitch the raw edges, taking a ⅝-inch (1.5 cm) seam allowance.

4 From pink patterned fabric and light sew-in interfacing, cut two 5¼ x 2¾-inch (13 x 7 cm) rectangles for the D-ring holders and one 30¼ x 5¼-inch (77 x 13 cm) strip for the strap. Baste the interfacing to the wrong side of the fabric pieces. With right sides facing, fold the D-rings in half, stitch the short edges, taking a ⅝-inch (1.5 cm) seam allowance.

5 Turn right side out and press in half. Slip a ring onto each D-ring holder. Turn the bag right side out. Pin the raw ends of the D-ring holders together and stitch to the upper edge of the bands over the seams, taking a ⅜-inch (1 cm) seam allowance.

6 With right sides facing, fold the strap lengthwise in half, stitch the long edges, taking a ⅝-inch (1.5 cm) seam allowance. Turn right side out and press. Turn ⅜-inch (1 cm) at each end to the inside. Baste in place. Slip the strap through the D-rings. Baste the pressed ends 1 inch (2.5 cm) above the D-rings. Stitch close to the pressed ends then ¼ inch (6 mm) from the first stitching.

7 Refer to the diagram on page 124 to cut two linings from pink patterned fabric. With right sides facing and taking a ⅝-inch (1.5 cm) seam allowance, stitch the side seams, leaving a gap in one seam to turn right side out. Press the seams open. Follow Step 3 to stitch the base. With right sides facing, insert the bag in the lining, matching the seams. Pin and stitch the upper edge, taking a ⅝-inch (1.5 cm) seam allowance.

8 Turn right side out. Slipstitch the gap closed. Press the lining to the inside. Topstitch close to the upper edge then ¼ inch (6 mm) below. Fold and pin the bag 1½ inches (4 cm) from the side and base seams. Topstitch ⁵⁄₃₂ inch (4 mm) from the folds, finishing ⁵⁄₃₂ inch (4 mm) from short seams at the ends of the base seams.

wall organizer

Encourage a well-organized workspace with this vibrant wall organizer. The pockets are pleated to provide storage for stationery or small toys. Stiffening the pockets with interfacing keeps the pleats sharp. The wall organizer measures 23 x 15 inches (59 x 38 cm); metal eyelets are fixed to the top so it can be hung on hooks.

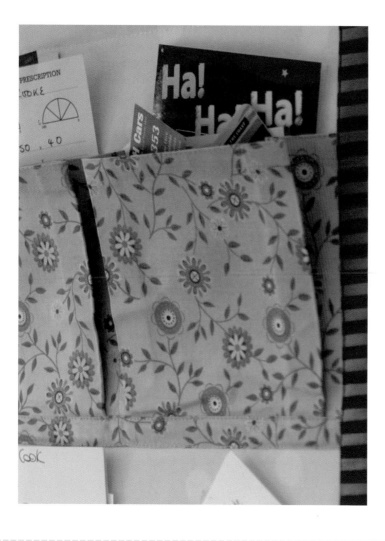

you will need

- ¼ yard (20 cm) each of 44-inch (112 cm) wide green patterned fabric, blue patterned fabric, and pink striped fabric

- matching sewing threads

- 1⅓ yards (120 cm) of 36-inch (90 cm) wide firm iron-on interfacing

- 1 yard (80 cm) of 54-inch (137 cm) wide yellow spotted fabric

- ¾-inch (18 mm) wide bias binding maker

- 12⅝-inch (2 x 32 cm) lengths of ¾ x ⁵⁄₃₂-inch (18 x 4 mm) half round stripwood

- 2 metal eyelets about ⅝ inch (1.5 cm) in diameter and eyelet cutter

- pin hammer

1 Cut one 23¼ x 7¼-inch (58 x 18.5 cm) strip of green and one of blue patterned fabric and two of interfacing for the pockets. Fuse the interfacing to the wrong side of the pockets. Press under ⅜ inch (1 cm) then ⅝ inch (1.5 cm) on the long upper edge. Stitch close to both pressed edges to hem the pockets.

2 With the pockets right side up, refer to the diagram on page 124 to make the pleats by bringing the solid lines to the broken lines. Press the pleats and baste across the lower edges. Cut one 28¼ x 15-inch (72 x 38 cm) rectangle of yellow spotted fabric and interfacing for the wall organizer. Fuse the interfacing to the wrong side of the wall organizer. Neaten the short upper and lower edges of the wall organizer with a zigzag stitch.

3 Pin the pockets to the wall organizer, with the upper edge of the green pocket 8⅝ inches (22 cm) below the upper edge of the wall organizer and the lower raw edge of the blue pocket 4⅝ inches (11.5 cm) above the lower edge of the wall organizer. Baste the side and lower edges of the pockets. To form the separate pockets, stitch between the center pleats.

4 Cut one 15 x 1⅜-inch (38 x 3.5 cm) straight strip of green and one of blue patterned fabric. Make a binding using an ¾-inch (18 mm) bias binding maker (see making bias binding technique, page 17). Pin and baste the binding over the lower edge of the pockets, matching the lower edge of the pockets to the center of the binding. Stitch close to both long edges of the binding.

5 Press under 3⅜ inches (8.5 cm) on the upper edge and 1⅞ inches (4.5 cm) on the lower edge of the wall organizer. On the right side, topstitch close to the pressed edges. Stitch 1½ inches (4 cm) then 1¼ inches (3 cm) below the upper edge. Stitch 1¼ inch (3 cm) above the lower edge. Insert a 12⅝-inch (32 cm) length of ¾ x ⁵⁄₃₂-inch (18 x 4 mm) stripwood through the 1¼-inch (3 cm) wide channels. Baste across the ends of the channels.

6 Cut two 24¼ x 3-inch (62 x 8 cm) straight strips of pink striped fabric for the side bindings. Press the bindings lengthwise in half with wrong sides facing. Open out flat and press the long edges to meet at the center. Press under ⅝ inch (1.5 cm) at each end of the bindings.

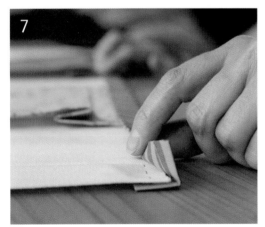

7 Slip one long edge of the wall organizer inside one binding. Baste through all the layers. Slipstitch the ends together enclosing the upper and lower edges of the wall organizer. Repeat on the other long edge of the wall organizer. Stitch close to the inner pressed edges of the bindings.

8 Fix a metal eyelet 1 inch (2.5 cm) inside each side edge at the top of the wall organizer using a pin hammer and following the manufacturer's instructions.

buttoned blind

Choose two pretty fabrics that work well together to make this neat button-up blind. A pair of loops at the bottom of the blind can fasten onto buttons along the side edges to raise the blind to different levels. The fabric quantities needed will depend upon the size of the blind.

you will need

- 44-inch (112 cm) wide turquoise patterned cotton fabric for blind front

- 44-inch (112 cm) wide green spotted cotton fabric for blind back

- matching sewing threads

- 1⅜-inches (3.5 cm) wide x ⁵⁄₃₂-inch (4 mm) thick strip wood batten

- sew-on hook and loop tape

- eight ⅞-inch (2.3 cm) buttons

- staple gun

2 Turn right side out with a bodkin and cut in half to make two button loops. Baste each button loop to the lower edge of the blind front on the right side, 1 inch (2.5 cm) in from the side edges with a ¾-inch (2 cm) gap within each loop.

1 Measure the intended width and drop of the blind. Cut a square or rectangle of both fabrics with ⅝ inch (1.5 cm) added to all edges for seam allowances. Cut a 6 x 1-inch (15 x 2.5 cm) wide bias strip of the blind back fabric for the button loops. Fold the strip lengthwise in half with right sides facing. Stitch the long edges taking ¼-inch (6 mm) seam allowance.

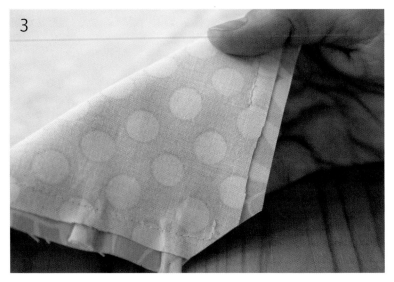

3 Pin the front and back blinds together with right sides facing. Taking a ⅝-inch (1.5 cm) seam allowance, stitch the side and lower edges, leaving a 1¾-inch (4.5 cm) gap ¾ inch (2 cm) above the lower edge in one side seam. Trim the seam allowances to layer them and clip the corners.

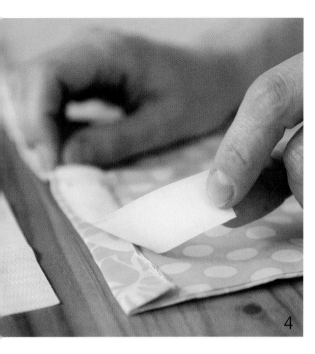

4 Turn the blind right side out and press it. Press under 1.5 cm) ⅝ inch (on the upper edge. Cut touch-and-close tape ¼-inch (6 mm) shorter than the width of the blind. Pull the tapes apart. Pin one tape to the upper edge of the blind ⅛ inch (3 mm) inside the upper and side edges. Stitch close to the edges of the tape.

5 Topstitch close to the lower edge then 2 inches (5 cm) above the lower edge to form a channel. Saw two pieces of strip wood ¼ inch (6 mm) shorter than the width of the blind. Insert one batten through the channel. Slipstitch the gap closed.

6 Divide the side edges into fifths and mark the divisions on each side edge with a pin. Sew a button at each division 1¼ inches (3 cm) in from the side edges. Screw the remaining wood batten above the window. Use a staple gun to staple the corresponding touch-and-close tape to the batten. Press the upper edge of the blind to the batten to fix in place.

lampshade

Transform a ready-made drum lampshade into a stylish new version trimmed with a border of flamboyant rouleau coils. If you are feeling adventurous, cover the entire lampshade with coils for a lavish effect.

you will need

- drum lampshade, approximately 8 inches (20 cm) tall x 10 inches (25 cm) in diameter

- Approximately 1¼ yards (1 m) of 36-inch (90 cm) wide turquoise linen

- matching sewing threads

- ½-inch (1.5 cm) bias binding maker

- fabric glue

- glue spreader

- rouleau turner (optional)

1 Measure the circumference and height of the lampshade. Cut a rectangle of linen to cover the lampshade that is the circumference measurement plus 1¼ inch (3 cm) x ¼ inch (6 mm) less than the height. Press under ½ inch (1.2 cm) on one short edge of the cover.

2 Starting at the seam of the lampshade, wrap the cover around the lampshade ⅛ inch (3 mm) below the upper edge. Smooth the cover around the lampshade and lay the pressed edge over the other end and pin in position. Slipstitch the pressed edge in place.

3 Cut two 1-inch (2.5 cm) wide bias strips measuring the circumference of the lampshade plus 1¼ inch (3 cm) in length for the bindings. Use the strips to make two lengths of bias binding using a ½-inch (1.2 cm) bias binding maker (see making bias binding technique, page 17). Press under one end of the bindings.

4 Apply glue sparingly to the raw end of one binding with a glue spreader. Starting at the lampshade seam, start to glue the binding around the lower edge of the lampshade, covering the lower raw edge of the cover. Continue spreading glue and sticking the binding in place. Repeat on the upper edge of the lampshade, allowing the binding to extend ⅛ inch (3 mm) above the lampshade.

5 Cut four 36-inch (90 cm) lengths of 1-inch (2.5 cm) wide bias strips for the rouleau. Fold one strip lengthwise in half with right sides facing. Stitch the long edges taking a ³⁄₁₆-inch (5 mm) seam allowance.

6 Turn the rouleau right side out with a bodkin or rouleau turner. Repeat to make the other rouleau. Poke in the raw ends of the rouleau with the ends of a pair of embroidery scissors. Turn the lampshade upside down.

7 Measure and divide the lower edge of the lampshade into quarters and mark each division with a pin. Within one marked section, pin one rouleau in random curling shapes around the lower edge of the lampshade. Take care to pin through the fabric only and not the lampshade.

8 When you are happy with the design, catch the rouleau to the fabric with small stitches. Remove the pins as you sew. Continue applying the rouleau around the lampshade.

cupcake doorstop

Here is an amusing project that is practical too. This larger-than-life cupcake is weighted to hold a door open. It's fun to make and can be decorated with beads as lavishly or as simply as you wish. If you cannot find turquoise jumbo corduroy, dye white or cream jumbo corduroy to achieve the color you want.

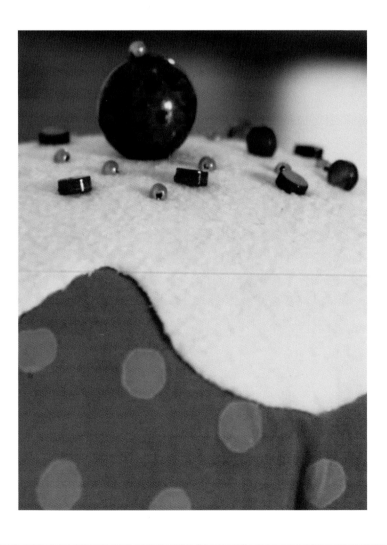

you will need

- ¼ yard (20 cm) of 36-inch (90 cm) wide turquoise jumbo corduroy

- 16-inch (40 cm) square of pink with orange spotted fabric

- matching sewing threads

- thin cardstock 3¾ inches (9.5 cm) in diameter

- 8-inch (20 cm) square of pale yellow fleece

- 2 pounds (1 kg) of rice

- approximately 2 ounces (50 g) polyester toy filling

- 1 inch (2.5 cm) pink bead

- approximately seven $\frac{5}{32}$-inch (4 mm) pale orange beads

- approximately seven $\frac{5}{16}$-inch (8 mm) pink disc beads

1 Use the template on page 126 to cut four bases from corduroy, matching the arrow to the ridges of the corduroy. With right sides facing and taking a ⅜-inch (1 cm) seam allowance, |stitch the bases together along the short edges, forming a ring. Press the seams open.

TIP Corduroy has a nap which means the surface has a pile and appears different from different angles, so cut all the base pieces in the same direction.

2 Cut a 4¾-inch (12 cm) diameter circle of corduroy for the bottom of the base. Fold the circle into quarters and mark each division at the circumference with a pin. Snip the seam allowance of the lower curved edge of the base. This will make it easier to stitch to the bottom piece. With right sides facing, pin the bottom to the snipped edge, matching the pins to the seams. Stitch, taking a ⅜-inch (1 cm) seam allowance. Snip the curves.

3 Use the template on page 125 to cut a cake from spotted fabric. Cut slits along the broken lines. With right sides facing, fold, matching the edges of the darts. Stitch the darts to the dots, taking ¼-inch (6 mm) seam allowance. Snip the curves. Press the seams open.

4 Gather the edge of the cake with a long stitch. With right sides facing, pin the cake and case together, matching seams to darts. Pull up the gathers and stitch, taking a ⅜-inch (1 cm) seam allowance. Turn the doorstop right side out through the slits.

5 Position the cardstock circle in the case on the base. Adjust the seam allowance to lie against the sides of the case. Pour the rice into the doorstop. Fill the rest of the doorstop with the toy filling. Ladder stitch the slits securely closed by bringing the edges of the slits together and working hand stitches over the joins.

6 Use the template on page 126 to cut the icing from fleece. Pin the icing on the cake, making sure that it covers the sewn slits. Hand stitch in place with tiny stitches around the edges of the icing.

7 Anchor a double length of sewing thread to the top of the icing. Thread on a 1 inch (2.5 cm) pink bead and a 5/32-inch (4 mm) pale orange bead. Insert the needle back through the first bead and pull the thread. Make a small stitch through the icing and repeat to secure. Sew the remaining beads at random to the icing.

Templates

Some of the projects in this book refer to templates and diagrams. Trace the templates onto tracing paper or enlarge on a photocopier as indicated. Remember to transfer any grain lines, fold lines, and other useful information.

UPPER EDGE

(CUT 2)

stationery folder (pocket) (page 44)
Increase template size by 110%

pocketed napkin (pocket) (page 60)

Shown at full size

bordered throw diagram (page 66)

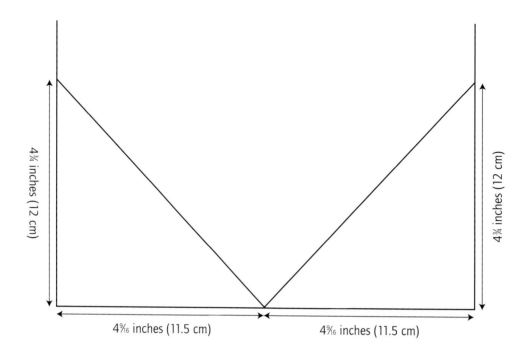

4¾ inches (12 cm)

4¾ inches (12 cm)

4⁹⁄₁₆ inches (11.5 cm)

4⁹⁄₁₆ inches (11.5 cm)

patchwork play mat (starfish) (page 68)
Shown at full size

UPPER EDGE

market bag (page 88)
Increase template size by 167%

FOLD

(CUT 2 PATTERNED)
(CUT 2 INTERFACING)
(CUT 2 DOTTED)

LOWER EDGE

16¾ inches (43 cm)

UPPER EDGE-LINING

UPPER EDGE-BAG

16¾ inches (43 cm)

SIDE SEAM

SIDE SEAM

14¾ inches (38 cm)

1½ inches (4 cm)

BASE SEAM

1½ inches (4 cm)

1½ inches (4 cm)

13¾ inches (35 cm)

1½ inches (4 cm)

beach bag diagram (page 100)

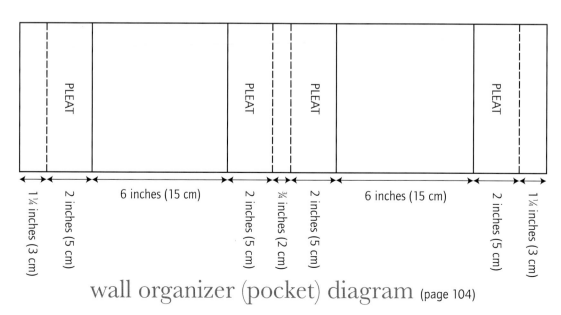

PLEAT

PLEAT

PLEAT

PLEAT

1¼ inches (3 cm)

2 inches (5 cm)

6 inches (15 cm)

2 inches (5 cm)

¾ inches (2 cm)

2 inches (5 cm)

6 inches (15 cm)

2 inches (5 cm)

1¼ inches (3 cm)

wall organizer (pocket) diagram (page 104)

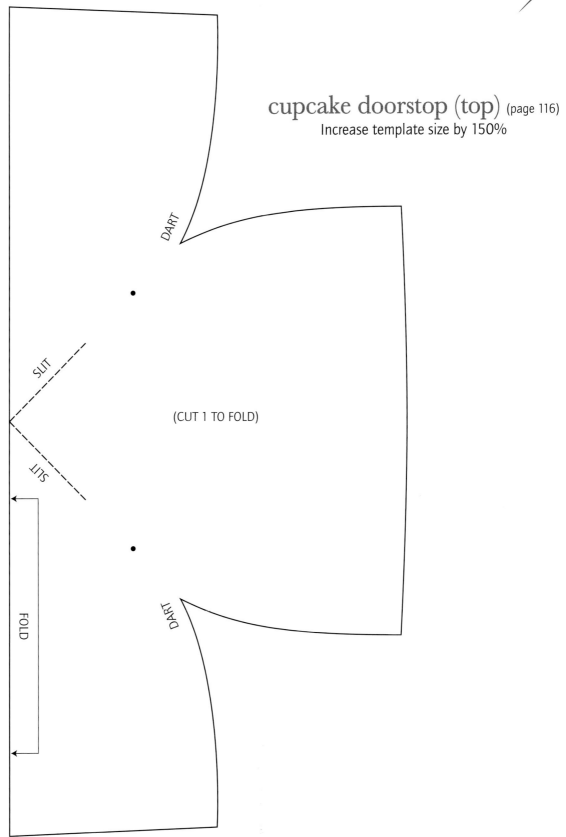

cupcake doorstop (top) (page 116)
Increase template size by 150%

DART

SLIT

SLIT

(CUT 1 TO FOLD)

FOLD

DART

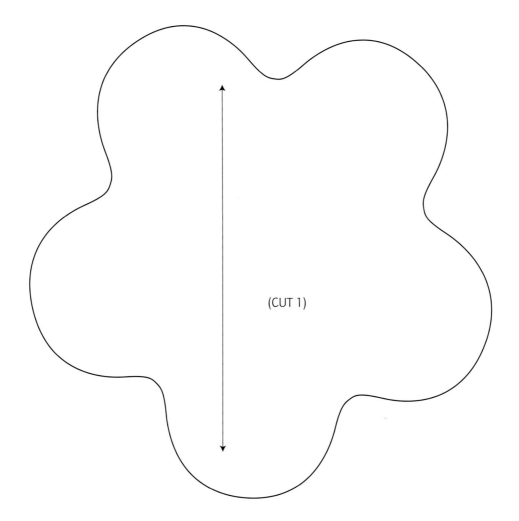

(CUT 4)

cupcake doorstop (base) (page 116)
Increase template size by 150%

(CUT 1)

cupcake doorstop (icing) (page 116)
Increase template size by 150%

Index

It's all on **www.larkcrafts.com**

Daily blog posts featuring needlearts, jewelry and beading, and all things crafty

Free, downloadable **projects** and **how-to videos**

Calls for artists and **book submissions**

A free **e-newsletter** announcing new and exciting books

...and a place to celebrate the **creative spirit**